THE OFFICIAL IRISH JO

Also in this series:

Edited by:
Peter Hornby

The Official Irish
Joke Book

Futura

A Futura Book

First published in Great Britain by
Futura Publications Limited in 1977
Reprinted 1978 (twice), 1979 (twice), 1980 (twice),
1981, 1982, 1983, 1985, 1987

ISBN 0 8600 7443 9

Printed and bound in Great Britain by
Hazell Watson & Viney Limited,
Member of the BPCC Group,
Aylesbury, Bucks

Futura Publications
A Division of
Macdonald & Co (Publishers) Ltd
Greater London House
Hampstead Road
London NW1 7QX
A BPCC plc Company

An Irish priest on a trip to Israel was horrified when quoted an outrageous price to be ferried across the Sea of Galilee. As he stalked off he was heard muttering, 'No wonder Jesus walked!'

* * *

An Irish conman went to New York but he didn't have a great deal of luck. The first man that he tried to sell the Brooklyn Bridge to turned out to be the owner and the Irishman had to pay him $50 so that he wouldn't tell the cops.

* * *

An Irishman on a building site was working at a tremendous rate. Every two minutes he dashed up a ladder with an enormous load of bricks. After this had been going on for an hour a friend asked why he was working so hard.

'Oh,' he said. 'Don't tell anyone but I've got them all fooled. I'm not really working hard at all – it's the same load of bricks every time!'

* * *

An eminent Irish archaeologist was giving a lecture in an American university.

'Some of the cities of the past,' he said sombrely, 'have vanished so completely that it's doubtful if some of them existed at all.'

* * *

An Irish intellectual has been defined as one who goes to a museum or art gallery when it isn't raining.

* * *

How do you recognize an Irishman in a car-wash? He'll be sitting on his bicycle.

* * *

Two young lads from the west coast took a trip to Dublin and while they were there they went to the cinema for the first time. The film had already started and the cinema was very dark and so the usherette walked down the aisle towards them with her torch.

'Look out,' said one of the lads to the other, 'there's a bicycle up ahead.'

* * *

You can always tell an Irish pirate. He's the one with a patch over each eye!

* * *

An American tourist was amazed at the speed with which a local was putting away Guinness in a Dublin pub and so bet him £20 that he couldn't drink ten pints in fifteen minutes. The Irishman asked for a few minutes to prepare and then left the pub. Twenty minutes later he came back and drank ten pints of Guinness in fifteen minutes. 'I knew I could do it,' he said, 'because I just did it in the pub down the road.'

* * *

An Irishman bought a washing machine for his wife on a new hire purchase scheme. 'It's a wonderful system,' he told her, '100 per cent down and nothing to pay each week.'

* * *

An Irishman bought his wife a pair of rubber gloves. When he asked her how she was getting on with them, she said, 'They're really very good. When you've got them on, sure, and you can wash your hands without getting them wet.'

* * *

Did you hear about the Irishman who was given a pair of cuff-links for his birthday?
He had no use for them – he couldn't find anywhere to get his wrists pierced.

* * *

An extremely unattractive Irishman claimed that he had been very beautiful as a baby but that he'd been exchanged by the gipsies.

* * *

An Irishman carrying two big bags of telephones was stopped at the customs in New York and asked what they were for.

'I don't know,' he said, 'I've just got a job with a small jazz band over here and they asked me to bring two sacks of phones with me.'

* * *

Then there was the Irish kidnapper who enclosed a stamped addressed envelope with the ransom demand.

* * *

After trying on caps for over half an hour, an Irishman turned to the shop assistant and said, 'Have you got one with a peak at the back?'

* * *

An Irish detective arrested a criminal and was about to handcuff him when a huge gust of wind blew the detective's hat off. 'Shall I go and fetch it?' the prisoner asked. 'Do you take me for a fool?' said the detective. 'You wait here while I go and get it!'

* * *

An Englishman met an Irishman limping along the road wearing only one shoe.
'What's up?' he asked. 'Lost a shoe?'
'No,' replied the Irishman. 'Just found one!'

* * *

A terrified Irishman was taking his first plane ride. He buckled himself in and a huge Scot, with a big, black beard sat down next to him. After take-off the Scot fell asleep. The poor Irishman was feeling extremely sick but was frightened to wake the slumbering giant next to him. Finally, he left it too long and was sick over the Scotsman. The Scotsman woke up and was amazed to see the mess all over his sporran and kilt.
'Do you feel better now?' asked the Irishman.

* * *

An Irishman arrived home from the pub early and found his wife in bed with another man. 'What on earth are you doing?' he shrieked. His wife looked at the man next to her and said, 'Didn't I tell you he was stupid?'

* * *

Did you hear about the really mean Irishman who fired his shotgun outside the backdoor on Christmas Eve? He went in and told his children that Father Christmas had committed suicide.

* * *

Two old Irishmen were sitting in the corner of what had been one of their favourite pubs – until it had been redecorated and the juke box put in.
'Ah, you know,' said one, 'I miss the old ways and the old days. I miss the sawdust, I miss the spittoon . . .'
'You always did,' said the other.

* * *

An Irishman was once hired by the managing director of a large bank to do some odd jobs around his house. When he got the bill he was furious.
'You're charging me £20 an hour. Why, I don't even earn that,' he said.
'Neither did I when I was managing director of a bank,' said the Irishman.

* * *

Did you hear about the Irish bank clerk who spent all his spare time sitting in a tree? He wanted to be a branch manager!

* * *

Then there was the Irishman whose sister had a baby. Nobody told him if it was a boy or a girl so he didn't know if he was an uncle or an aunt.

* * *

An Irish hen was so exasperated with one of her impish chicks that she said, 'If your father could see you now he'd turn in his gravy.'

* * *

An Irishman who was fed up with being bothered by hitch-hikers solved the problem. Whenever he drove out of town he just put up the notice 'TAXI'.

* * *

Did you hear about the Irishman who gave a lift to a beautiful young witch. They hadn't gone a few miles when she touched him on the knee and he turned into a lay-by.

* * *

An Irish lawyer was once asked what the penalty for bigamy was. 'Two mothers-in-law,' he replied.

* * *

Irishman: Sir, I wonder if you could let me off work tomorrow as my wife wants me to go shopping with her?
Boss: Certainly not. We're very busy.
Irishman: Thank you, sir. You're very kind.

* * *

Old Irishman: And then there was the time I was attacked by five hungry lions . . .
Young man: Oh, come on, grandad. Last time you told me that story, it was three lions!
Old Irishman: I know, but then you were too young to be told the whole frightening truth.

* * *

A vacuum cleaner salesman went to a very remote farmhouse on the west coast of Ireland and, before the woman of the house could object, started throwing all manner of dirt on the carpet.

'Madam,' he said, 'I have so much confidence in this machine that if this carpet is not spotless after it's been over it, then I will eat all the dirt that's left.'

'Well, you'd better start eating,' chuckled the woman, 'we haven't got the electricity yet.'

* * *

Irishman: Whenever I see you, you always remind me of that Welshman, Jones.

Scot: But I'm not at all like Jones.

Irishman: Oh, yes, you are! You both owe me £10!

* * *

An Irishman put 10 pence into the collection at church one Sunday. 'What,' he asked the young priest standing by the plate, 'happens to all this money?'

'It goes to the Lord,' answered the priest.

'Oh, well,' said the Irishman, removing his 10 pence from the plate, 'I'm seventy-five years old and I'm bound to see the Lord before a young man like you, and I can give it to him personally.'

* * *

An Irishman was asked to answer a riddle by the barman in his local.

'My mother gave birth to a child: it's not me sister and it's not me brother. Who is it?'

The Irishman cudgelled his brains but finally he had to admit defeat.

'It's me,' laughed the barman.

Thinking what a good riddle it was, the man put it to his wife when he got home. She too cudgelled her brains but couldn't work it out. And finally she too gave up.

'It's Jack, the barman in the Rose and Crown,' hooted the Irishman.

*　　*　　*

An old Irishman was bragging about his longevity, 'I'm eighty-three years old and I've never smoked, gambled, drank or looked at a woman in all that time.' His young grandson looked up sadly and said, 'I can't think why you wanted to live for so long.'

*　　*　　*

A blind man was sitting with a bowl begging in a Dublin Street. A woman threw a 10 pence piece at the bowl but it missed and rolled into the gutter. Before the astonished woman could say anything the blind man got up and retrieved the coin.

'I thought you were blind!' said the outraged woman.

'Oh, no. I'm not blind at all,' said the man, 'I'm standing in for the real blind man, who's gone to the cinema.'

*　　*　　*

Then there was the Irishman who was so broke that he got a visit from the blood bank because his blood had bounced.

* * *

An Irishman had been going on at great length about how wonderful his wife was, and how happy he was. Finally, one of the listeners, fed up, said, "Surely, she must have some faults!'
The Irishman thought very hard for a few minutes and then said, 'Well she does have a tendency to use foul language when she's drunk.'

* * *

An Irishman was telling a neighbouring farmer about his sick cow and the farmer told him that when his cow got sick he dosed her with arsenic. When the Irishman got back he dosed his cow with arsenic – and she died.
He stalked off to see his friend, who said, 'That's funny. So did mine.'

* * *

Funny how all newspaper stories about Irish social events seem to begin: Among the injured were...

*   *   *

Do you know the difference between baloney and blarney? To tell a woman of forty-five that she looks like a young girl is baloney. To ask her how old she is, so that you'll know at what age a woman looks her best, is blarney.

*   *   *

An Irishman opened a newspaper and was amazed to read his own obituary. Much amused he telephoned his best friend who asked him where he was ringing from...

*   *   *

An Irishman's mother-in-law passed on and his wife asked him what sort of gravestone they should get her.
'Something very, very heavy,' he replied.

*   *   *

A very tall man wearing a cowboy hat was on an Aer Lingus flight to Shannon. The stewardess asked him if he'd like a drink and he replied:
'Sure would, a whisky. By the way, the name's Brown: B-R-O-W-N. I'm from Texas, I'm six feet six inches tall. I'm white from my head to my toes and I hate the Irish.' The stewardess smiled warily and gave him his drink. As he was sipping it he turned to the man sitting next to him and said: 'The name's Brown: that's spelt B-R-O-W-N. I'm from Texas, I'm six feet six inches tall. I'm white from the top of my head to the tips of my toes and I hate the Irish.' The man looked at him for a moment and then said, 'How do you do? My name is Patrick O'Reilly. I'm from Dublin and I'm five feet five inches tall. I'm white from the top of my head to the tips of my toes – apart, that is, from my rectum which is brown. Spelt B-R-O-W-N.'

*   *   *

The priest was giving one of his parishioners his usual lecture. 'Abstinence,' he said, 'is a wonderful thing, Patrick.'
'Sure and I know it is, Father,' said Patrick, 'if practised in moderation.'

*   *   *

The magistrate was giving judgment:
'Young man,' he said sternly, 'it is alcohol and alcohol alone that is responsible for your appearance before this bench.'
'I'm very glad to hear you say that, your honour,' said the young Irishman. 'Everyone else says it's me own fault.'

* * *

When her husband fell out of the window of a high rise building to his death, Mrs O'Reilly collected a very large sum from the insurance company. But then came the lawyers, relatives, bills etc., and she was in such a state that the doctor was called. 'Sometimes,' she said to him, 'I almost wish that me husband hadn't fallen out of the window.'

* * *

How can you tell when an Irish invalid is getting better?
When he tries to blow the foam off his medicine.

* * *

Two very drunk Englishmen were arguing about whether or not the orb beaming from the heavens was the sun or the moon. An Irishman came lurching towards them and one of the Englishmen said, 'Say, sir, is that the sun or the moon up there?'

'I'm afraid, I don't know,' replied the Irishman, 'I'm a stranger here meself.'

* * *

O'Reilly was a little bit maudlin and turned to his best friend and said, 'I'd like you to promise me, Eamonn, that when I'm dead and buried you'll pour a bottle of good Irish whiskey over me grave.'

'Sure, and I'll do that,' answered his friend. 'Would you have any objections to it passing through my kidneys first?'

* * *

First Irishman: I always like to go to O'Reilly's birthday and help him drink up his presents.

Second Irishman: I don't really drink myself. I just gargle with whiskey and sometimes it slips down.

* * *

An Englishman walked into a bar in Dublin and said to the barman, 'That's so quaint – putting sawdust on the floor.'

'That isn't sawdust,' answered the barman, 'that's yesterday's furniture.'

* * *

The judge looked angrily down at the prisoner in the dock, 'Why,' he asked, 'did you kick and punch this man so brutally?'

'Sure, and it was all a terrible mistake, your honour. I had alcohol taken and was a little confused. I thought it was me wife.'

* * *

One of O'Reilly's friends asked him why he no longer wore glasses.

'I read so much about the evils of drinking,' he replied, 'either I had to give up drinking or I had to give up reading.'

* * *

First Irishman: O'Reilly does other things besides drink.
Second Irishman: Like what?
First Irishman: Well, he hiccups.

* * *

First Irishman: Me uncle fell down two flights of stairs with a crate of Guinness and he didn't spill a drop.
Second Irishman: How on earth did he manage that?
First Irishman: He kept his mouth closed.

* * *

First Irishman: Would you say that O'Reilly drinks a lot?

Second Irishman: I wouldn't say so. I think he drinks to calm himself.

First Irishman: Well, that would explain it. Last night he was so calm he couldn't move.

* * *

O'Reilly was very drunk and clambered unsteadily on to a bus. He lurched along it before sitting next to a priest.

'I'm not going to heaven,' he sighed. 'I'm not going to heaven. I'm not going to heaven because there is no heaven.'

'Well, go to hell then,' said the priest. 'But be quiet about it.'

* * *

Advertisement in a Dublin newspaper: Secondhand tombstone for sale. Ideal for person named O'Reilly.

* * *

21

A medical officer asked the sergeant in charge of a squad of Royal Irish Fusiliers what precautions he took against contaminated water.

'Well,' said the sergeant, 'first of all we boil it and then we filter it, sir.'

The M.O. nodded his approval.

'And then, sir,' continued the sergeant, 'just for safety's sake, we all drink beer.'

* * *

An Irish jeweller rang up the police in a terrible state. 'I've just been robbed by an elephant,' he managed to blurt out.

'What sort?' asked the duty sergeant. 'An Indian elephant with short ears or an African elephant with big ears?'

'How should I know?' answered the jeweller. 'He had a stocking over his head.'

* * *

An Irishman went to see a psychiatrist. 'Doctor,' he said, 'can I ask you just two questions?'

'Of course,' said the psychiatrist.

'Well, is it possible for a man to fall in love with an elephant?'

'No, it is not,' replied the psychiatrist. 'What is your second question?'

'Do you know anyone who needs a very large engagement ring?'

* * *

Two Irishmen were partners in a jewellery shop and one day they were lunching together. 'Oh my goodness,' said one, 'we left the safe unlocked!' 'What are you worried about?' asked the other. 'We're both here, aren't we?'

*　　*　　*

A young Irish lass was on the underground in London and a young English gallant asked her if she would like to sit down.
'No thank you,' she said, 'I'm in a fearful hurry.'

*　　*　　*

An Irishman had for many years been carrying on an affair. Finally, his wife confronted him with the fact.
'So what,' he laughed. 'And do you know, I have to meet the little darling this evening. And do you know who is going to help me get dressed? You are. And do you know who is going to shine my shoes? You are. And do you know who is going to tie my tie?'
'Yes,' said his unfortunate wife. 'The undertaker.'

*　　*　　*

'An Irishman was sitting in a pub wearing one blue sock and one red sock.

'That's a strange pair of socks you've got on,' said a friend.

'Yes it is,' he replied. 'And do you know, I've got another pair at home just like it.'

* * *

One day an Irish housewife went crazy. She broke up her kitchen completely and had to be taken away. Her husband was absolutely mystified:

'She's always been such a decent, hardworking woman,' he told his friends in the pub. 'Why, she hasn't been out of the kitchen in twenty years.'

* * *

Priest: What evil could possibly be worse than drink?

Parishioner: Thirst?

* * *

An old Irishman collapsed while crossing a busy Dublin street. Immediately he was surrounded by lots of people with all sorts of suggestions about how to revive him.

One old lady said, 'Give him some whiskey.' But she was completely ignored. Finally, the old boy opened his eyes and said, 'Will you all shut up and listen to that sweet old lady over there.'

*   *   *

A young Irish labourer emigrated to America. While wandering around New York he found his way into a bar which had a big notice saying, 'All the beer you can drink for $1.' Seeing this the Irishman said, 'All right, barman, I'll take two dollars' worth of that.'

*   *   *

A drunken Irishman noticed a man coming out of a supermarket with two heavy bags of shopping. 'Look at that!' he said to a passer-by. 'Going in there, wasting his money. I'm willing to bet he hasn't got a drop of booze in the house.'

*   *   *

'Drinking doesn't affect me at all,' boasted a big, tough Irishman. 'Take last night for instance, I drank twenty pints of porter and sixteen whiskeys and I felt fine. The only trouble was that people kept treading on my fingers.'

* * *

How can you tell if an Irishman is an aristocrat? His tattoo has no spelling mistakes in it.

* * *

There was an advertisement for a man who was sober, reliable and could drive. Dutifully, O'Reilly went off to apply. The man asked him, 'Can you drive?'
'No,' answered O'Reilly.
'Do you drink?' asked the man.
'Indeed I do,' answered O'Reilly.
'Then why,' asked the man, 'did you answer the advertisement?'
'I just wanted to tell you that I'm not reliable,' answered O'Reilly.

* * *

As the train left the station three Irishmen went racing along the platform and two of them jumped on, leaving their mate stranded, laughing his head off.

'What are you laughing at?' asked one of the porters.

'Those two,' said the man. 'They came here to see me off.'

*   *   *

A policeman saw an Irishman sitting on top of an oak tree and asked him what he was doing up there.

'I don't know,' said the man, 'I think I must have sat on an acorn.'

*   *   *

An Englishman was boasting about his scarecrows. 'They were so good this year that not a single bird came anywhere near our farm.'

'That's impressive,' said an Irishman, 'but ours were so good this year that the birds brought back the corn they stole last year.'

*   *   *

A man with more than a touch of the blarney about him went into a restaurant and said to the waitress, 'A steak, a salad and a kind word.' The waitress went away and a short while later returned with his order.

'What about the kind word?' he asked. She bent over and whispered in his ear, 'Don't eat the steak.'

* * *

An Irishman, noted for his tall tales, was telling a tourist about how hot it had been the summer before. 'Why,' he said, 'I saw a fox being chased by the hounds one day and it was so hot they were all walking.'

* * *

How do you recognize an Irish pencil? It's got a rubber at both ends.

* * *

What do you do if an Irishman throws a pin at you? Run like hell – he's probably got a grenade between his teeth.

* * *

What do you do if an Irishman throws a grenade at you? Take out the pin and throw it back.

* * *

Two Irish furniture removers once spent thirty minutes wrestling with a heavy wardrobe that was wedged on a landing.

'It's no good,' said one, 'we'll never get it upstairs.'

'Upstairs,' said the other one, 'I thought we were trying to get it downstairs.'

* * *

An old Irishman went from Dublin to the west coast for his health. He hadn't been back two days when he died. Two of his friends were looking at the open coffin.

'Doesn't he look wonderful?' said one of them.

'He certainly does,' said the other. 'That month in the country must have done him the world of good.'

* * *

Two Americans went into a bar in Dublin and asked for Guinness. 'Make sure the glass is clean,' said one. The barman poured their drinks. 'Two pints,' he announced after a while. 'Who asked for the clean glass?'

* * *

Two Irishmen were walking down the road when they saw a human head on the pavement. 'Hey,' said one, 'that looks like O'Reilly.' 'No,' said the other one. 'O'Reilly was much taller than that.'

* * *

The Irish space programme has run into a technical hitch: The astronaut keeps falling off the kite.

* * *

How do you make an Irish cocktail? Put a potato in a pint of Guinness.

* * *

Did you hear about the Irish terrorist who tried to blow up a bus? He burnt his mouth on the exhaust pipe.

* * *

Two Irishmen were in a plane when the captain announced that one of the engines had conked out and that the flight would be delayed a little, although it was perfectly safe. Two more times the captain made the same announcement, and the third time one of the Irishmen said to the other, 'If that last engine goes, we could be up here all night.'

* * *

An Irishman showed up at his girl-friend's house with water dripping from his shirt. 'What's the matter?' she asked. 'Why is your shirt dripping wet?'

'Oh,' said the Irishman, 'It says on the label "wash and wear".'

* * *

A gorilla escaped from the zoo and adopted an Irishman who was minding his own business. A policeman went over to the Irishman and asked him what was going on.

'I don't know,' said the Irishman.

'Well,' said the policeman, 'you'd better take that gorilla to the zoo.'

The Irishman nodded and walked off with the gorilla holding his hand.

The next day the same policeman was astonished to see the Irishman and the gorilla walking along the road again.

'Hey,' said the policeman, 'I thought I told you to take that gorilla to the zoo.'

'I did,' said the Irishman, 'and he enjoyed it so much, I'm going to take him again this afternoon.'

* * *

Mrs O'Reilly went into her son's bedroom and said, 'Come on, it's 7.30. Time to get up and go to school.'
'But I don't want to go to school.'
'Don't be silly, dear.'
'But I really hate school, mother. The kids don't like me, the teachers don't like me. Even the janitor doesn't like me.'
'Come on, get up,' said Mrs O'Reilly, 'you've got to go – you're the headmaster.'

* * *

The Irish navy asked for all the lighthouses to be turned upside down, so that their submarines wouldn't get lost.

* * *

What is the first thing you learn from an Irish piano teacher? How to move the piano.

* * *

Police now have indisputable proof that an Irish Mafia exists. Some weeks ago two men were found with their heads tied together, shot through the hands.

* * *

An Irishman went to his doctor for advice on improving his sex life. After examining him, the doctor recommended that he jog five miles every day for a week and then ring him. A week later, the Irishman telephoned.

'Has the jogging improved your sex life?' asked the doctor.

'I'm not sure,' said the Irishman, 'I'm thirty-five miles from home.'

*   *   *

Priest: Do you want to go to Heaven?

Irish Parishioner: No, Father.

Priest: But you must want to go to Heaven when you die.

Irish Parishioner: Oh, yes, when I die, Father. I thought you were getting a party together now.

*   *   *

Why do haircuts cost £4 in Ireland? The charge is £1 per corner.

*   *   *

An Irishman filled in a job application. The personnel manager looked down the form and then said, 'I see that your birthday is on March 17. What year?'

'Oh, every year,' replied the Irishman.

*   *   *

An Irishman once moved after hearing that 90 per cent of road accidents occur within three miles of home.

* * *

Teacher: What is an autobiography?
Irish pupil: The story of a car?

* * *

Mrs O'Reilly: Eamonn's teacher says he ought to have an encyclopedia.
Mr O'Reilly: What for? Let him walk to school like I had to.

* * *

Did you hear about the dairy farmer who made all his cows sleep on their backs? He wanted the cream to be on top in the morning.

* * *

Did you hear about the Irish prostitute who was once found picketing the do-it-yourself show at Olympia?

* * *

Or about the pregnant Irish girl who hired two private detectives to find out if the baby was really hers?

* * *

One very hot day in June an Irish house painter was seen by his boss sweltering in two jackets. 'What have you got two jackets on for?' his boss asked.
'Oh,' said the painter. 'It says on the tin "Put on two coats".'

* * *

O'Reilly's mother went round to see him one day, looking like thunder. 'Why do you never call me on the telephone?' she demanded.

'Mother,' said O'Reilly, 'you don't have a telephone!'

'I know that,' she said. 'But you do.'

* * *

A shaky Irish barber once managed to cut a man three times while shaving him. The third time the man asked for a razor. 'What for?' asked the barber. 'Do you want to shave yourself?'

'No,' answered the man, 'I want to defend myself.'

* * *

'I never have to worry about my wife going off with other fellows,' bragged O'Reilly. 'She's a wonderful, kind, considerate woman. And very very ugly.'

* * *

O'Reilly went to see the parish priest. 'Father,' he said, 'before I die, I'd like to convert to Protestantism.'

'Why on earth do you want to do that?' asked the astonished priest.

'Well, surely you don't want to lose a good Catholic when I die, do you?' said O'Reilly.

* * *

Did you hear about the Irish girl who believed in long engagements? She was pregnant six months before she got married.

*　　*　　*

Or the newly married Irish girl who wrote off to the army for all her husband's favourite recipes!

*　　*　　*

Or the Irish farmer who gave his sheep iron pills so that he would get steel wool?

*　　*　　*

Or about the brand new parachute designed by an Irishman? It opens on impact.

*　　*　　*

Or even about the Irish ventriloquist who was so dim that finally his dummy left him?

*　　*　　*

A giant of a man walked into a Dublin pub with a tiger on a lead. He looked fiercely round the bar and then yelled at the barman, 'Do you serve Englishmen in here?'

'Of course, sir,' said the apprehensive barman.

'Good,' said the man, 'I'll have two for the tiger.'

*   *   *

There was once an Irishman with a terrible inferiority complex. He thought everybody else was as good as he was.

*   *   *

An Irishman walked into a bar with a pig under his arm. 'Where on earth did you get that?' asked the barman.

'I won him in a raffle,' said the pig.

*   *   *

A young Irish girl was hired as a secretary and on her first day the phone rang. She answered it and hung up almost immediately. This happened three or four times and finally her boss asked her who was ringing.

'Oh,' she said petulantly, 'some fool who keeps telling me it's a long distance from New York.'

*   *   *

An Irish mountaineering expedition was unsuccessful in its assault on Everest. It ran out of scaffolding just a few feet short of the summit.

*   *   *

Two Irishmen each had a horse but they had great difficulty in telling them apart, so one of them docked his horse's tail. Everything was splendid, but then the second horse had a nasty accident and he unfortunately lost his tail. And the two men found themselves back at square one. They decided to consult a famous professor to see if he could help them. He looked at the two horses for a while and then said, 'It's really very easy, that bay mare is about half a hand bigger than that grey stallion.'

*   *   *

A man went into a barber's shop holding a small boy by the hand. After the man had had a haircut, shampoo and shave, he placed the boy in the chair. 'I'm just going to buy a bottle,' he said, 'I'll be back in a minute.'
The boy had his haircut and the man hadn't returned. 'Looks like your daddy's forgotten all about you,' the barber said to the boy.
'Oh, that wasn't my dad,' said the boy. 'He just walked up to me outside and said, 'Come on, son, let's go and have a free haircut.'

*   *   *

A woman had stalled her car at a set of traffic lights in Dublin. The lights kept changing . . . Red . . . Yellow . . . Green . . . Finally a policeman came up to her and leant nonchalantly into the car, 'What's the matter, lady?' he asked. 'Haven't we got any colours you like?'

* * *

Two Irishmen were having a fierce argument about whether or not the English have a sense of humour. One of them ended the dispute once and for all when he said, 'The English have a tremendous sense of humour: they laugh three times at every joke: once when they hear it, once when it's explained to them, and once when they understand it.'

* * *

A priest went to see O'Reilly in hospital. 'I'm going to pray,' he said, 'that you'll forgive McCann for hitting you with that bottle.'
'There's no need to waste your time, Father. Wait till I get better, and then pray for McCann.'

* * *

Two Irishman hijacked a submarine. They demanded a million dollars ransom and two parachutes.

* * *

Paddy was on his death bed, about to breathe his last, when he smelt some of his wife's cooking. He beckoned weakly to his son and told him to ask the good lady for a plate of her delicious ham so that he could die a happy man. The boy raced off and returned a few seconds later and said, 'Ma says to tell you not to be so silly, she's saving that ham for the wake.'

* * *

Why do Irish dogs have flat faces?
From chasing parked cars.

* * *

The American tourist was bragging in a Dublin bar about American technology.
'Who was it that put a man on the moon?' he asked.
'That's not so great,' said the barman. 'We Irish are planning to put a man on the sun.'
'You can't do that. He'll be frazzled to a crisp before he's anywhere near the sun,' said the American.
'Oh, no,' said the barman. 'We'll be sending him at night.'

* * *

A man was in tears at Lime Street Station in Liverpool. A woman asked him what was the matter. 'I've just come over from Ireland,' he sobbed, 'and I've lost all me luggage.'
'That's terrible,' said the woman. 'What happened?'
'Oh,' he said. 'The cork came out.'

* * *

How do you recognize an Irish hippy?
Flared wellingtons.

* * *

An Irishman was very worried about his wife and so he went to see a psychiatrist about her. 'She's got this terrible fear of having her clothes stolen,' he said. 'Why, only the other day I got home early and found that she'd hired a man to stay in the wardrobe to guard them.'

* * *

O'Reilly was arrested for murder but bribed a member of the jury to hold out for manslaughter. The jury was out for eight hours, but when it returned the verdict was manslaughter. O'Reilly smiled at the man he'd bribed and whispered, 'I'm really very grateful, I hope it wasn't too difficult.'

'It was touch and go,' said the man, 'the others all wanted to acquit you.'

* * *

Did you hear about the Irishman who called his pet zebra 'Spot'?

* * *

A young lad up from the country spent a day in Dublin and on his return regaled his friends in the pub with tales of derring-do.

'Why, it's a great city,' he said. 'Do you know I'd not been there an hour when I was befriended by this charming lady who took me back to her apartment. As soon as we got there, do you know, she took off all her clothes. Why, I think if I'd played my cards right, I could've kissed her.'

* * *

A man walked into a pub in London and asked the barman if he'd heard the latest Irish joke.

'I'd better be warning you,' said the barman, 'I'm Irish meself.'

'That's O.K.,' said the man, 'I'll tell it slowly.'

*   *   *

An Irishman looked up from his newspaper and said to his wife, 'I'll never understand how it is that people always die in alphabetical order.'

*   *   *

The doctor had finished his examination of the strapping Irish navvy and said, 'Well, there's nothing seriously wrong with you, but I think you ought to give up drinking the hard stuff, and try to drink at least one pint of milk a day.'

'But, Doctor,' said the navvy, 'milk's awfully dangerous stuff. Why, a friend of mine was killed by drinking milk.'

'How on earth did that happen?' asked the doctor.

'Well, Doctor, the cow fell on him.'

*   *   *

Two Irishmen were working on a building site when a large chunk of steel fell on one's head and cut off his ear.

'Don't worry, Joe,' said the other, 'I'll search among the rubble and find it and the surgeon can sew it back on again.'

After about five minutes he found the ear and brought it back triumphantly.

'You fool,' Joe shouted, 'that's not my ear. Mine had a cigarette behind it.'

* * *

O'Reilly had too much drink one fair day and he accidentally broke a pane of glass in a shop window. When he saw what he had done he sobered up a bit and started to run for all his worth. Unfortunately a policeman saw him and gave chase, and finally caught up with him.

'Now,' he said, 'you're not going to get away with that. I saw you breaking the window and then running away.'

'I wasn't running away, sir,' said O'Reilly. 'I was only running home to get the price of it to repay the owner.'

* * *

A fire broke out in Paddy's bedroom and the insurance people hesitated to pay up as they had reason to believe that Paddy was drunk, and carelessly smoking, thereby setting fire to the bed himself.

Paddy answered their charge by swearing that he was as sober as a judge and that the bed was actually on fire when he got into it!

*   *   *

Then there was the Irish boy who was asked at school how he would divide twenty potatoes among six people. He said he'd boil them and mash them.

*   *   *

An Irish couple began to learn Swahili because they had just adopted a black baby boy and they wanted to be able to understand him when he started to speak.

*   *   *

Irishman to shoemaker, 'You stupid fool. I told you to make one shoe bigger than the other and instead of that you have made one smaller than the other.'

*   *   *

American Tourist: Our farms are so big that if you started to plough a furrow in spring by the time you had got to the end of it you could harvest the crop on the way back.

Irishman: That's nothing. In Ireland if a young married couple went out to milk the cows the children would bring back the milk.

* * *

'How far is it from here to the hotel?' asked an English tourist.

'It's about a fifteen-minute walk,' answered an Irish local, 'if you run like hell.'

* * *

There was the Irishman who was always boasting how happily married he was. He told everyone the secret of his marriage was that his wife made all the minor decisions, while she allowed him to make all the major ones.

'What decisions, for example, do you make?' asked a cowed listener.

'Oh, I decide on how to solve the problem of the North; whether to give Rhodesia back to the blacks, whether we should leave the Common Market, and such like important problems.'

* * *

Two men were sitting on a wall outside the mental home in Dublin. One had a long piece of stick that he was casting towards the middle of the road and reeling in as if he were fishing. A passing policeman looked at him for a while and then went over to the other man and said:

'Is this fellow out of the mental home?'

'Oh, he is,' answered the other.

'Well take him back there as quickly as you can.'

'O.K. Hey, Jack, reel in and I'll row home.'

* * *

Then there was the Irishman who heard an hilarious story but wouldn't bring it home since he thought that would be carrying the joke too far.

* * *

An Irishman was working on a building site and one week he got £2 too much in his wages. He kept very quiet about it. In the meantime the error was noticed and £2 was deducted from his wages the next week. He went up to the cashier and complained angrily.

'You didn't complain too much last week when you got £2 too much,' said the cashier.

'Once is one thing,' said the Irishman, 'but when a mistake happens twice a man has a right to complain.'

* * *

An Irishman was once asked why they built the railway station two miles from the town. He answered:

'Well, they thought it would be a good idea to have the station near the railway.'

*　　*　　*

Then there was the Irishman who sent a cheque for £50 to his aunt as a birthday gift, but he didn't sign it as he didn't want her to know who sent it.

*　　*　　*

An Irish farmer was on holiday in Dublin. He complained to the bell-boy: 'I'm not going to have this room. You couldn't swing a cat in it. It's no better than a pigsty and I'm not going to sleep in a miserable folding bed. Don't think that because I'm from the country you can fool me.'

'Get in, sir,' said the boy, 'this is the lift.'

*　　*　　*

Judge: 'Speeding again? How many times have you been before me?

Irish Defendant: 'Never, Your Worship. I tried to pass you on the road twice but my car will only do sixty-five.'

*　　*　　*

An Irish farmer went on his honeymoon to London and was angered to find twin beds in the hotel room.

'What's upsetting you?' asked the shy bride.

'I thought we were going to have a room to ourselves,' answered the farmer.

* * *

Irishman to St Peter at the Golden Gates:

'You must be bored with your job showing people in year after year, century after century?'

St Peter: 'You must remember, here in Heaven things are measured differently. A million years are but as one minute; a million pounds are but as one shilling.'

Irishman: 'Could you loan me a shilling, Holy Saint?'

St Peter: 'Certainly – in a minute!'

* * *

Then there was the Irishman whose car was painted green on one side and grey on the other. He loves to hear witnesses contend with each other.

* * *

Old man a bit bewildered at very fashionable wedding:

'Are you the bridegroom?'

Irishman: 'No, sir, I was knocked out in the semi-finals.'

* * *

Waiter to Irishman: 'Will you have red or white wine, sir?'

Irishman: 'It's all the same to me. I'm colour blind.'

* * *

An Irishman was riding his bicycle with no light and was stopped by a policeman.

'What's your name?' asked the policeman.

'John Smith.'

'That can't be your name. Give me your real name.'

'Well,' said the Irishman, 'you can put me down as William Shakespeare.'

'That's better,' said the policeman. 'You can't fool me with the "Smith" nonsense.'

* * *

Boss: 'You've already had time off for your mother-in-law's funeral, for your child's measles, for your son's first communion. What is it now?'

Irishman: 'I'm getting married, sir.'

* * *

There was the Irish woman who fell overboard in shark-infested waters. The sharks didn't touch her because they were 'man-eating'.

*   *   *

Then there was the Irishman who used to snore so loud that he'd wake himself up. But he cured himself. He sleeps in the next room now.

*   *   *

An Irishman was given a pair of water skis for his birthday by his wife. Some months later when he still hadn't used them she asked him why not and he told her that he couldn't find a lake with a slope.

*   *   *

You can always tell an Irishman on an oil rig. He's the one throwing bread to the helicopters.

*   *   *

The police in Dublin uncovered a very large-scale fraud. It seems that a group of Dubliners had forged thousands of pounds worth of 10p pieces by cutting the corners off 50p pieces.

*   *   *

Two Irishmen were sent to gaol and were given the same cell. One of them asked the other how long he was in for and was told, 'Eight years.'

'Oh,' he said. 'Well, you'd better take the bed by the door. I'm in for ten, so you'll be leaving before me.'

* * *

A very rich Texan was sitting in a bar in Dublin and as he got drunker so he got louder and more boastful about his home state. 'In Texas,' he drawled, 'a man can get on a train on Monday morning, eat and sleep on that train all through Monday and all through Tuesday. And when he gets off that train on Wednesday, he's still in Texas.'

The barman looked up and shook his head, 'Sure, it's terrible,' he said. 'We've got slow trains in Ireland too.'

* * *

After O'Reilly had jumped a red light and smashed into another car, he dashed over to the other vehicle to discover that the driver was a priest. 'Good God, man, you almost killed me,' said the badly shaken priest.

'I'm really sorry, Father. Here,' said O'Reilly, taking a bottle from his pocket, 'Drink some of this whiskey, for your nerves.'

The grateful priest gulped down some of the whiskey and then started shouting again. 'What do you think you were doing? I'm lucky to be alive.'

'Oh, Father, I'm so sorry. You'll feel a lot better after you've drunk some more of this.'

The priest had a few more stiff belts and then asked, 'Why don't you have a drink?'

'I don't think I will, thank you, Father,' said O'Reilly. 'I'll just sit here and wait for the police.'

*   *   *

It was Sunday and there was an expectant hush in the church as the priest mounted the steps of the pulpit. He looked sadly down at his flock and then said, 'Today, I'm going to demonstrate to you the evils of the demon drink.' He then placed two glasses on the pulpit and pulled a worm out of his pocket. 'In the first glass, water,' he said and dangled the worm in the glass. He then took the worm out of the glass and said triumphantly, 'The worm is still alive.' He paused and then continued, 'In the second glass, whiskey,' and placed the worm in that. After a few seconds he took the worm out of the whiskey and said, 'The worm is dead.' He paused again and then said in a tired voice, 'Now, what is it that I'm trying to tell you?' A little fellow at the back of the church got up and said, 'If you please, Father, you're trying to tell us that if you drink whiskey you won't get worms.'

*　　*　　*

An Irishman rushed into a police station and told the duty sergeant that his car had just been stolen. 'Did you get a look at the thief?' the sergeant asked.
'No,' said the Irishman, 'but I got his number.'

*　　*　　*

A little Irish village had just bought a new fire engine and the local councillors were wondering what should be done with the old one.

'Why not keep the old engine for false alarms?' asked one old councillor.

*　　*　　*

Have you heard about the Irishman who sold a £10 parking ticket to a Scot for £5?

*　　*　　*

An Irishman read about experiments showing that the tar and nicotine in cigarettes caused cancer in rats and mice. Deeply moved, he put all his cigarettes on the top shelf where the rats and mice couldn't get at them.

*　　*　　*

An Irishman went to America where he became a policeman. One night he had handed out a hundred and seventy-three parking tickets before he realized that he was at a drive-in movie.

*　　*　　*

How do you recognize an Irish racing driver in a big race? He makes a hundred pit stops. Three for fuel, four for tyre changes, and ninety-three to ask for directions.

* * *

How do you recognize a well-mannered Irish-man?
He doesn't blow his soup – he fans it with his cap.

* * *

Have you heard about the Irishman who went to a mind reader?
He got his money back.

* * *

What about the Irish grandmother who went on the pill?
She didn't want to have any more grandchildren.

* * *

Have you heard about the Irishman who thought that manual labour was a Spanish trade union official?

* * *

Then there was the Irish helicopter pilot who crashed.
He thought it was too cold so he turned the fan off.

* * *

An Irishman was sitting on his front doorstep dressed in pyjamas and dressing gown at three o'clock in the morning when a policeman passed by.
'What are you doing here?' asked the policeman.
'I'm waiting for the cat to come home, so I can put him out for the night,' said the Irishman.

* * *

Have you heard about the Irish explorer who paid £10 for a sheet of sandpaper?
He thought it was a map of the Sahara Desert.

* * *

An old lady asked an Irish tramp why he was dressed in such a miserable collection of rags.
'It's a medical condition,' he told her. 'There isn't a tailor in town who can measure me for a suit, I'm that ticklish.'

* * *

An Irishman who was 4 feet 6 inches tall offered his services to a circus. He claimed he was the tallest dwarf in the world.

* * *

There once was an Irish medical student who failed all his exams in surgery because he couldn't lance a boil properly.
He kept falling off the horse.

* * *

How can you recognize a superstitious Irishman? He won't work during any week with a Friday in it.

* * *

The following sign is displayed prominently in an Irish shop:

CREDIT IS GIVEN ONLY TO THOSE OVER EIGHTY – PROVIDED THEY ARE ACCOMPANIED BY THEIR GRANDPARENTS.

* * *

Have you heard about the Irishman who got a job as quality control officer in a banana factory?
They had to sack him because he kept throwing away all the ones that were crooked.

* * *

An Irishman once wrote to the Guinness Book of Records and claimed that he should be included. He explained that at one time he had been the youngest person in the world.

*   *   *

Have you heard about the Irishman who bought a black and white dog?
He thought the licence would be cheaper than for a coloured one.

*   *   *

How do you recognize an aircraft designed by an Irishman?
It has outside toilets.

*   *   *

Have you heard about the Irishman who took up water polo?
His horse got drowned.

*   *   *

'Gentlemen of the jury,' shouted the crier in an Irish court, 'please proceed to your accustomed places.'
The court erupted as the twelve Irishmen proceeded to rush towards the dock.

*   *   *

An Irishman saw a lobster pot for the first time and having been told what it was called, exclaimed, 'I don't believe it. How would you get a lobster to sit on one of those things?'

*　*　*

There was an Irishman who thought that aperitif was the French for a set of dentures.

*　*　*

An Irish lawyer whose client was charged with murdering his father and mother by chopping their heads off with an axe opened his defence as follows:
'Gentlemen of the jury, consider this poor orphan...'

*　*　*

What do you find written on the bottom of Irish beer bottles?
Open other end.
What do you find written on the top of Irish beer bottles?
See other end for instructions.

*　*　*

How do you recognize a roll of Irish toilet paper?
Look for the instructions printed on every sheet.

*　*　*

Have you heard about the Irish girl who came second in a beauty contest?
She was the only entrant.

* * *

How does an Irishman do a 'Spot the Ball' entry?
He prods around his newspaper with a pin until he hears 'psst'.

* * *

How many Irishmen does it take to carry out a kidnapping?
Ten – one to capture the kid and nine to write the ransom note.

* * *

Have you heard the sad story of the Irishman who was a haemophiliac?
He tried to cure himself by acupuncture.

* * *

How do you recognize an Irish cuckoo clock?
Every twenty-five minutes the cuckoo pops its head out and asks the time.

* * *

How do you sink a submarine designed by an Irishman?
Put it in water.

* * *

An Irishman joined the army and after three years' service was awarded the special crossed knife and fork insignia. This was to celebrate three years of eating with a knife and fork without accident.

* * *

An Irishman was on his first visit to the zoo. He was annoyed because he followed the sign LADIES but they were all locked in their cages where he couldn't see them.

* * *

An Irish traffic warden explained the system of yellow lines on city streets as follows:
One yellow line means no parking at all.
Two yellow lines mean no parking at all at all.

* * *

Two Irishmen were waiting at a bus stop. When the bus arrived it turned out to be a one-man bus, so one man turned to the other and said:
'You can take this bus, I'll wait for the next one.'

* * *

Have you heard about the Irishman who decided to have only three children?
He heard that one in every four children born is Chinese.

* * *

How do you recognize an Irishman staying in a fancy hotel?
He's the one trying to slam the revolving door.

* * *

Have you heard about the Irishman who thought that Chou-en-Lai was Chinese for bed and breakfast?

* * *

Have you heard about the Irishwoman who was ironing her husband's socks?
She burned his feet.

* * *

Have you heard about the Irishman who thought that a barbecue was a line of people waiting outside a gents hairdressers?

* * *

How can we be sure that Santa Claus is an Irishman?
There are two doors in the average house and eight windows and he goes down the chimney.

*　　*　　*

Have you heard about the Irishman with a serious problem?
He thought he had a bigger and better inferiority complex than anybody else in the world.

*　　*　　*

'I hear that your husband had a post-mortem operation,' said one Irishwoman to another. 'Yes,' replied the second; 'but not until after he was dead. If only they had done it a bit earlier it might have saved his life.'

*　　*　　*

An Irishman explained the fact that cream is more expensive than milk as follows:
Cream is dearer because they find it harder to make the cows sit on the smaller bottles.

*　　*　　*

What goes putt-putt-putt-putt . . .?
An Irish golfer.

*　　*　　*

Why do Irishmen make the best secret agents? Even under torture they can't remember what they have been assigned to do.

*   *   *

Two Irishmen kidnapped a little Irish boy. Two days after the kidnapping they sent the little lad home to his parents with a ransom note. The next day the parents sent him back with the money.

*   *   *

Have you heard about the Irishman who joined the Mafia?
They made him an offer he couldn't understand.

*   *   *

'How did Mrs O'Sullivan's appendix operation go?' an Irish doctor was asked by his nurse.
'Appendix operation?' he screamed. 'I was told it was a post-mortem.'

*   *   *

An Irishman was being charged with driving down the middle of the road. In defence he stated that one of the instructions in his driving test application form had been 'tear along the dotted line'.

*   *   *

An Irishman who was fined £10 for being drunk and disorderly told the judge that he had no money.

'You would if you hadn't spent it on drink,' the judge told him.

*   *   *

Why do Irish workers never go on strike?
Nobody would notice the difference.

*   *   *

Have you heard about the Irishman who never took his wife out anywhere?
His mother had warned him not to go out with married women.

*   *   *

Have you heard about the Irishman who spent three hours in a carwash?
He thought it was raining too hard to drive.

*   *   *

An Irishman was thrilled with his genuine Rembrandt.
'It's one of the few works he did in ballpoint,' he told his friends proudly.

*   *   *

An Irishman invented a cure for seasickness – sit under a tree.

*   *   *

An Irishman was asked for names for his sister's newly born twins, a boy and a girl. He suggested Denise and Denephew.

*   *   *

Have you heard about the Irishman who lost £10 on the Grand National?
Then, he lost £15 on the action replay.

*   *   *

Then there was the Irishman who made a fortune by taking up a collection for the widow of the Unknown Soldier.

*   *   *

Have you heard about the Irishman who cut a hole in his umbrella?
He wanted to know when it stopped raining.

*   *   *

In what month do Irishmen drink the least Guinness?
February.

*   *   *

How do you recognize an Irish intellectual?
He doesn't move his lips when he reads.

*   *   *

Why are Irish jokes so simple?
So the English can understand them.

*   *   *

Why is the wheelbarrow the greatest of all human inventions?
It taught the English to walk on their hind legs.

*   *   *

How do you tell the age of an Irishman?
Cut off his head and count the rings.

*   *   *

Why do so many Irishmen have scratched faces?
From trying to eat with forks.

*   *   *

An Irishman went to a library and asked the librarian if he could recommend any plays for him to read.

'How about Shaw?' said the librarian.

'I'll give him a try,' answered the Irishman, so the librarian handed him *The Complete Plays of George Bernard Shaw*.

Next day he returned saying he had finished the book and had enjoyed it very much.

'Do you have any more plays by the same author?' he enquired.

For a joke, the librarian gave him a telephone directory to take home, and when the Irishman returned two days later the librarian asked him if he had enjoyed it.

'Well,' said the Irishman, 'I didn't think much of the plot, but what a cast.'

* * *

A man was giving an Irishman a lift in his car but he wasn't sure if his indicators were working. So he asked the Irishman to go behind the car and tell him.

'Well,' he shouted after a few seconds, 'are they working?'

'They are, they aren't, they are, they aren't,' replied the Irishman.

* * *

Two poteen makers were on their first train journey. With them they had a pint bottle of poteen. As the first man raised the bottle to his lips and took a long drink, the train passed through a tunnel.

'Don't touch that stuff,' he yelled to the second man, 'I've just been struck blind.'

*　　*　　*

An Irishman went to a psychiatrist and told him that his wife thought she was a television set.

'Don't worry,' said the psychiatrist, 'I'll soon cure her of that.'

'Oh I don't want her cured,' said the Irishman, 'just tune her in to BBC1.'

*　　*　　*

An Irishman arrived home early one afternoon and as he came in the door the telephone rang so he answered it.

'Who was that on the phone?' shouted his wife from the dining-room.

'It was a wrong number, darling,' said the Irishman, 'some fellow looking for the Met. Office. He wanted to know if the coast was clear.'

*　　*　　*

An Irishman was explaining the mysteries of science and telecommunications to his small son. 'The telephone,' he told him, 'is like a huge dog with his tail in London and his head in Dublin. When you tread on his tail in London he barks in Dublin.'

'That's wonderful,' said the small boy, 'now tell me about the radio.'

'The radio is exactly the same,' said the Irishman, 'but without the dog.'

* * *

An Irishman's coat fell down a sewer and he spent half an hour trying to get it out again.

A passerby suggested that he abandon the coat because even if he retrieved it, it would never be fit to wear again.

'Oh I know that,' said the Irishman, 'but there were four sandwiches in the pocket.'

* * *

Two Irishmen were talking in a Dublin pub.

'I wouldn't go to America if you paid me,' said the first.

'Why?' said the second.

'Well for one thing, they all drive on the right-hand side of the road there.'

'And what's wrong with that?' said the second man.

'Well I tried it driving to Dublin the other day and it's terrible.'

* * *

An Irishman who lived in a remote mountain village was awakened one morning by the postman delivering a letter.

'You shouldn't have come all that way just to bring me one letter,' he said. 'You should've posted it.'

* * *

An Irishman was condemned to receive forty lashes but the more they whipped him the more he laughed.

'Why are you laughing?' they asked him.

'You don't understand,' he told them, helpless with laughter, 'you're whipping the wrong man.'

* * *

An Irishman got a position as assistant in a hotel kitchen and was given the job of filling all the salt cellars. After a few hours he was asked if he had finished but replied that he had only managed to fill one.

'It's the devil's own job putting the salt in through that little hole at the top,' he added.

* * *

An Irish travel agent noticed an old lady and old man gazing longingly at his display of posters for exotic holiday resorts. As a publicity gimmick he decided to offer them a free round-the-world cruise with all expenses paid.

When they returned some months later he asked the old lady if they had enjoyed themselves. 'Wonderfully,' she replied, 'but tell me one thing, who was that old man I had to sleep with every night?'

*　　*　　*

An Irishman got a job working in a storeroom and the first assignment he was given was to put THIS END UP labels on a couple of hundred crates.

A little later, when asked if he had managed to do it, he answered, 'Yes, and in case they couldn't be seen on the top, I've put them on the bottom as well.'

*　　*　　*

An old Irishman and his wife were on a visit to Dublin, and decided to have a meal at an expensive restaurant where they ordered a four-course dinner with steak as the main course. When the meal was served the Irishman tucked in hungrily while his wife sat looking at her plate for over ten minutes.

'Isn't the meal to madam's satisfaction?' asked the head waiter.

'Certainly it is,' said the old lady with relish, 'but I'm waiting for Pa to finish with the teeth.'

*　　*　　*

A successful Irish business man was boasting about how poor his family had been when he was a child.

'For the first five years,' he claimed, 'I hadn't a stitch to wear. Then when I was six my father bought me a cap and I used to sit looking out the window.'

* * *

An Irishman was lecturing about his travels in foreign countries. 'I came across a strange custom among the Chinese,' he told his audience. 'If a rich man was condemned to death, he could save his life by paying somebody to die in his place. Many of the poor people made their living by acting as substitutes in this way.'

* * *

An Irishman sent his son to university and after a while the lad was awarded his B.A. On graduation he received the following telegram from his father:

'Congratulations on your B.A. Now for the other 24 letters and this time try to get them in the right order.'

* * *

An Irish newspaper once printed the following notice on its front page:

'Today we present our prize crossword, first prize £1,000. But those of you who want to do it just for fun and don't want to wait until next week for the answers, you can find the solution on the back page.'

* * *

A pilot in a single-seat jet fighter once ran into trouble when flying over Dublin. Seeing that his aircraft was on fire, he used the ejector seat to bale out. Two farmers were looking up at the scene, and one turned to the other and said, 'Mick, what will they think of next? I'm sure that was a flying toasting machine.'

* * *

Two Irish labourers wandering aimlessly across their site were asked by the foreman what they were doing.

'We're carrying these bricks to the other end of the site,' they told him.

'What bricks?' he asked them.

'Will you look at that,' said one Irishman to the other, 'we've forgotten the bricks.'

* * *

An Irishman, more than a little drunk, arrived home in the early hours of the morning wondering how he could get up the stairs to bed without waking his wife. Suddenly he had a bright idea. Tying all the pots and pans he could find to a piece of string he proceeded to drag them upstairs. 'She'll never hear me with all this noise,' he laughed.

* * *

Two Irishmen wanted to make some easy money so they bought a truckload of turnips at tenpence each. They sold the turnips at tenpence each and when they counted the proceeds they were amazed to find that they had exactly the same amount of money as they started with.
'See,' said the first man to the other, 'I told you we should have bought a bigger truck.'

* * *

An Irishman on a visit to Dublin decided to send a surprise birthday gift to his wife at home, so he rang Interparrot and asked them to send her a parrot that could speak seven languages. When he arrived home he found that she had plucked the parrot and roasted it. 'You fool,' he screamed at her, 'that bird spoke seven different languages.' 'Well why didn't he say something before I put him in the oven?' she asked.

* * *

One Irishman was trying to explain to another some of the basic theory of thermodynamics. 'Heat expands and cold contracts,' he told him.
'I understand perfectly,' said the other man, 'how else could you explain why the days are longer in summer and shorter in winter?'

*　　*　　*

Three Irishmen were caught up in the French Revolution and were sentenced to be guillotined. As the first man waited for the blade to fall, it stuck, and he was released according to the old custom. The same thing happened to the second man and he too was released.
As the third man looked up waiting for the blade to fall he shouted out, 'Hold on, I think I can see what's making it stick.'

*　　*　　*

An Irishman walked into a pub with a front door under his arm.
'Why are you carrying that door?' asked the barman.
'Well,' said the Irishman, 'last night I lost the key, so in case anybody finds it and breaks into my house I'm carrying the door around.'
'But what happens if you lose the door?'
'That's O.K.,' said the Irishman, 'I've left a window open.'

*　　*　　*

An Irishman got a job on a building site but the foreman was not very satisfied with the amount of work he was doing. One afternoon he found the man digging in a pit. He ordered him out of the pit and he did so.

'Now get back in again,' he told him. After he'd done it six or seven times the Irishman said, 'Look, what the hell are you playing at?'

'That's better,' said the foreman, 'you're taking more out on your boots than you were throwing out with your shovel.'

* * *

An Irishman telephoned the police and asked them to come straight away because the steering wheel, the gear lever, the clutch, the brake and the accelerator of his car had all been stolen.

A few minutes later he rang back and told them not to bother because he had got into the back seat by mistake.

* * *

An Irishman was in court charged with stealing a horse.

'You have a choice,' the judge said. 'You can be tried by me alone or by a jury of your peers.'

'What do you mean by "peers"?' asked the Irishman.

'Peers are your equals, men of your own kind and class.'

'Try me yourself then,' said the Irishman, 'I don't want to be tried by a bunch of villains.'

* * *

An Irishman and a Scotsman were taking an intelligence test.

'What bird does not build its own nest?' asked the examiner.

'The canary,' said the Scot, 'he lives in a cage.'

'The cuckoo,' said the Irishman.

'Very good,' said the examiner to the Irishman. 'How did you know?'

'Everybody knows the cuckoo lives in a clock,' said the Irishman.

* * *

An Irishman was charged with murder but was acquitted. Afterwards he told his lawyer that he could prove he was innocent because he was in jail at the time the crime was committed.

'Why on earth didn't you tell that to the court?' asked his lawyer.

'I thought that it might prejudice the jury,' said the Irishman.

* * *

An Englishman went to live in Dublin but unfortunately died. Two Dubliners went around from house to house collecting money to give him a decent funeral.

'Excuse me, sir,' they asked one old Dubliner, 'would you contribute £1 to bury an Englishman?'

'Look,' said the Dubliner, 'here's £10 – bury ten of them.'

* * *

An Irishman went to a concert and had to listen to a ventriloquist tell Irish joke after Irish joke. Finally, he'd had enough and rose to his feet, shouting, 'Listen, I'm fed up with these Irish jokes. What makes you think we're all that stupid?'

The ventriloquist smiled and said, 'Please, sir, would you sit down. These are only jokes and I've never met an Irishman yet who didn't have a sense of humour.'

'I'm not talking to you,' raged the Irishman, 'I'm talking to the little fellow on your knee.'

* * *

Why are there only 20 hours in an Irish day?
Have you ever seen an Irishman with 24 fingers and toes?

* * *

Did you hear about the Irishman who's wife wanted a coat made of animal skin?
He gave her a donkey jacket.

* * *

How can you tell an Irishman in Holland?
Wooden wellies.

* * *

An Irishman signed in at a London hotel. The manager noticed that the signature was XX and mentioned to the man that he found it puzzling. 'Oh, there's no need to be puzzled,' said the Irishman. 'The first X stands for Patrick Maguire, and the second X stands for B.A.'

*   *   *

Did you hear about the Irishman who kept his budgie in a goldfish bowl? A friend asked him why he didn't put it in a cage, like everyone else. 'I tried that,' he said, 'but the water kept coming out.'

*   *   *

An Irishman arrived home very late one night with a black eye and a painful looking swelling on his left cheek. 'And what might have happened to you?' asked his wife. 'Well,' he said, 'I had a little set-to with that small German fellow who lives down the way.' 'What,' yelled his wife, 'why are you letting a sawed-off little runt of a man do that to you?'
'Oh, now, be quiet,' he said. 'You shouldn't be disrespectful of the dead.'

*   *   *

Did you hear about the Irishman who went to the dentist to have a wisdom tooth put in?

*   *   *

An Aer Lingus pilot was asked for his height and position and replied, 'I'm five feet four and I'm in the front seat.'

*   *   *

Have you heard about the Irishman who went on the Generation Game and won a pair of sliding doors and a conveyor belt?

*   *   *

A commercial traveller was passing through a small town in Ireland when he saw a sumptuous funeral going past. 'Who's died?' he asked a passer-by.
'I'm not sure,' replied the local, 'but I think it's the one in the hearse.'

*   *   *

What does an Irishman wear in the summer?
Peep-toed wellies.

*   *   *

How do you keep an Irishman happy for an afternoon?
Write P.T.O. on both sides of a piece of paper.

*   *   *

A crusty old lady went on holiday and asked her Irish neighbour to look after her goldfish. On her return she asked him if he had changed the water. 'I most certainly have not,' he replied. 'They didn't drink what I gave them last week.'

*　　*　　*

An Irish love poem:

The tender young love of a beautiful girl,
And the love of a strong young man,
And the love of a mother for her child,
Have gone on since time began.
But the greatest love, the love of loves,
Even greater than that of a mother,
Is the all-consuming infinite love
Of one Irish drunk for another.

*　　*　　*

The captain of an Aer Lingus jet is identified by the three gold rings on his wellies.

*　　*　　*

How do you tell an Irish solicitor?
Pin-striped donkey jacket and charcoal-grey wellies.

*　　*　　*

An Irishman fell fifty feet and was asked if the fall had hurt him, 'No,' he said, ''twas the abrupt stop.' He thought for a moment or two and then said, 'I was actually rather lucky that the ground broke my fall.'

*　　*　　*

An Irishman was mugged in New York but put up a terrific fight before yielding his wallet, which contained $5? 'You put up a fight like that for $5?' asked his attackers incredulously.
'No,' he moaned, 'I thought you were after the $100 I've got hidden in my left shoe.'

*　　*　　*

An Irishman visited the zoo and was much taken by the kangaroos. A friend asked him what was so fascinating and he pointed at the notice that read 'A native of Australia' and said proudly, 'My sister married one.'

*　　*　　*

How do you brainwash an Irishman?
Fill his wellies full of water.

*　　*　　*

An Irishman in New York was looking at the Empire State Building when a conman approached him. 'I'm sorry,' said the conman, 'but I'm afraid it's a dollar for every storey you look at.'

'Oh,' said the Irishman, 'I only looked at 5.' And he gave the conman $5. He smiled at a bystander when the conman had gone, 'I fooled him,' he said, 'I was really looking right at the top.'

* * *

Did you hear about the Irishman who got a job sweeping leaves in St James's Park? He fell out of the tree and broke his leg.

* * *

Why wasn't Jesus Christ born in Ireland?
They couldn't find three wise men or a virgin.

* * *

An Irishman went into a hardware store and bought two dozen mothballs. The next day he went in again and asked for another two dozen. 'But you bought two dozen only yesterday,' said the assistant.
'I know,' said the man, 'but those moths are very hard to hit.'

* * *

How do you recognize an Irish firing squad?
It forms a circle.
How can you tell if the prisoner is Irish?
He doesn't duck.

* * *

An Irishman went to the cinema. He bought his ticket and then went in to see the film. A few minutes later he appeared at the box office and bought another ticket. A few minutes later he went to the box office again and asked for another ticket.
'What's the idea?' asked the cashier. 'I've already sold you two tickets.'
'I know,' he said, 'but every time I try to get in, some bloke keeps tearing them up.'

* * *

How do you recognize the bride at an Irish wedding?
She's the one in the white wellies.

* * *

Two Irishmen were walking by a nudist colony and decided to look in, so one stood on the other's shoulders to look over the wall. 'Are there men *and* women in there?' asked the one at the bottom. 'I can't tell,' said the one on his shoulders, 'they haven't got any clothes on.'

* * *

A small Irish town decided to build a bridge and the council was debating its construction.

'Which side of the river,' asked one portly councillor, 'has the most traffic?'

'The south side,' answered the clerk.

'Splendid,' said the councillor,' then that must be the side we build the bridge on.'

* * *

How do you get an Irishman to burn his face?
Telephone him while he's ironing.

* * *

Did you hear about the Irish housewife who had an accident while ironing the curtains?
She fell out of the window.

* * *

An Irishman wanted to marry a Welsh girl but her parents forbade it, so the unhappy couple decided to jump off Beachy Head.
Only the girl hit the water though – the Irishman got lost on the way down.

* * *

An Irishman consistently arrived late for work until his long-suffering boss asked him what was wrong.

'My problem,' explained the Irishman, 'is that I sleep very slowly.'

*   *   *

'What did the doctor say?' asked the anxious friend of an Irishman.

'He told me I must give up the drink and restricted me to one glass a day.'

'Did he now?'

'He did,' said the Irishman. 'Right now, I'm halfway through 1987.'

*   *   *

Two Irishmen staggered into a bar. One of them ordered two double whiskeys and watched while his friend drank his in one swallow, swirled around and then keeled over.

'That's what I like about John,' he said to the barman, 'he knows when he's had enough.'

*   *   *

The priest asked O'Reilly why he drank.

'Booze killed me mother,' said O'Reilly, 'and booze killed me father. I'm drinking for revenge.'

*   *   *

A small town in Ireland had a poster printed:
Help Support your Local Police:
Bribe Them.

* * *

Did you hear about the Irishman who killed himself by jumping off a tower block after his foreman told him that he used to fly Wellingtons during the war?

* * *

Or about the Irishman who thought that Royal Enfield was where the Queen kept her chickens?

* * *

And then there was the Irish tap dancer who fell in the sink.

* * *

There was an Irish literary critic who entered the debate about who wrote Shakespeare's plays declaring, 'They were not written by Shakespeare but by another gentleman of the same name.'

* * *

Then there was the Irishman who set his jacket alight because he wanted a blazer.

* * *

Did you hear about the Irishman who took his car for a service but couldn't get it in the church door?

* * *

A young Irish lad sat in the confessional and began his confession, 'Forgive me, Father, for I have sinned. I have committed the sin of fornication with one of the women of the parish.'
'And who, pray, was it?' asked the priest.
'I'm afraid I can't betray her,' answered the lad.
'Was it Margaret O'Reilly?' asked the priest.
'It was not.'
'Well then was it Kathleen McBride?'
'I'm afraid, Father, I cannot answer,' said the lad and fled from the church. Outside, he ran into one of his friends.
'Did the Father absolve you?' asked his friend.
'No, he did not,' replied the lad, 'but he did give me two good leads.'

* * *

The priest was selling tickets for a church social and accosted a recalcitrant member of the public. 'I'm afraid, Father, that I'll not be able to attend, but my spirit will be with you,' said the man, intending to walk on.

'That's fine,' said the priest, 'does your spirit want a £1 or a £2 ticket?'

* * *

A young Irish priest, just out of the seminary, went to a very lazy parish on the west coast. After an uneventful month he went into the church one day and was stopped in his tracks for, kneeling at the altar, there was Jesus Christ. The young priest raced off to collect his superior, who came back with him. When they arrived back in the church there, sure enough, was Jesus. 'What shall we do?' whispered the young priest. His superior looked thoughtful for a moment and then said, 'Look busy.'

* * *

Two comely nuns were walking past a roadworks when great brawny hands seized them by the ankles and hauled them into the trench, and then the two of them were raped. As they climbed out of the hole and smoothed down their habits one of them turned to the other and said tearfully, 'What are we going to tell Mother Superior? Raped twice in the same day.'

'What do you mean twice?' asked her companion.

'We are going back the same way, aren't we?' asked the first.

*　　*　　*

An Irish priest was sent as a missionary to a tribe of cannibals. He made great progress; in no time at all he had convinced them that on Fridays they should only eat fishermen.

*　　*　　*

Did you hear about the Irishman who was walking down the road punching women, kicking dogs and cursing children?

He was on his way to confession and didn't have much material.

*　　*　　*

One Sunday, an Irish priest was delivering his usual doleful sermon. 'One day,' he intoned morosely, 'every man in this parish will die.' He was somewhat amazed to see a man in the back row chuckling. He looked at the man sadly and said, 'Why is it that you're laughing when I say that one day everyone in this parish will die?'

The man continued chuckling and said, 'I'm not from this parish!'

*   *   *

Another priest was breathing fire and brimstone. 'Stand up, I say, stand up, all of ye who prefer sin,' he positively boomed and startled a man who had been sleeping in the back row and who leapt to his feet. 'So you,' roared the irate priest, 'actually prefer sin?'

'Oh, I'm sorry, Father,' answered the man, 'I thought you said gin.'

*   *   *

A drunk staggered out of a bar in Dublin straight into the arms of a priest. 'Drunk, is it?' said the priest. 'When are you going to learn what evils the drink is responsible for?'

'Father,' asked the drunk, 'what is it that causes the arthritis?'

'I'll tell you what it is,' thundered the priest, warming to his task, 'it's drinking water of Guinness, betting on the horses and consorting with loose women. How long have you had the arthritis?'

'Oh, I haven't got the arthritis,' said the man, 'but the bishop has!'

*   *   *

Yet another priest was haranguing his parishioners: 'The drink has killed millions, it rots their stomachs and they die in agony. The smoking has killed millions. It coats their lungs and they too die in agony. Overeating and consorting with loose women have also killed millions...'

'I'm sorry to bother you, Father,' piped a thin voice from the back, 'but what is it that kills the people who live right?'

*   *   *

Two nuns were walking along a dark alley when they were grabbed and raped.

'Oh, Father, forgive them,' cried one, 'for they know not what they do.'

'Shut up,' said the other, 'this one certainly does.'

*   *   *

Kathleen, a young Irish lass, fell in love with Simon, a good Jewish boy. Her father told Simon that if they wanted to marry, then the lad would have to become a Catholic.

For a year he studied very hard and learnt all he could about Catholicism and every Sunday he went to church.

Then one day Kathleen went tearfully to her father and told him that Simon wasn't going to marry her.

'Why not?' asked her father. 'He was getting on very well with our religion.'

'That's the problem,' she sobbed, 'Simon has decided to become a priest!'